# *Historic* SCOTLAND

## 5000 YEARS OF SCOTLAND'S HERITAGE

DAVID J BREEZE

FOREWORD BY

HRH THE PRINCE CHARLES, DUKE OF ROTHESAY

BT BAISFORD LTD/HISTORIC SCOTLAND

Text © David J. Breeze

First published 1998

All photographs © Historic Scotland

Map on page 126 by Michelle McCluskie

Designed by DWN Ltd, London

Printed in Singapore

Published by B. T. Batsford Ltd
583 Fulham Road, London SW6 5BY

A CIP catalogue record for this book is available
from the British Library.

ISBN 0 7134 8394 6

**Front Jacket**: Kilchurn Castle, Loch Awe, Argyll
**Back Jacket**: Smailholm Tower in the Borders
**Opposite page**: The Crypt of Glasgow Cathedral

Batsford On Line Archaeology and Architecture titles
**www.batsford.com**

# LIST OF CONTENTS

Rothesay Castle. The title of Duke of Rothesay was first created in 1398 to honour Prince David, the eldest son of Robert III. The title has been held by the sovereign's heir ever since.

4

ST. JAMES'S PALACE

Scotland has a unique built heritage going back over 5,000 years. The great prehistoric tomb of Maes Howe in Orkney and the brochs of the north and west are eloquent testimony to the engineering and building skills of our distant ancestors. The mysterious stones carved by the Picts before the last Millennium remain not only enigmatic, but strangely evocative of a lost world. The disturbed conditions of the later middle ages have furnished us with many tower-houses - a particular Scottish contribution to defence. In later centuries industrialisation has changed the landscape yet again and many fine examples remain of the buildings erected to serve this new master.

David Breeze has woven these tangible records of our past into a story which relates the history of Scotland through its buildings. Over 80 fine photographs illustrate ancient monuments and historic buildings from Shetland to the Solway, and from the Western Isles to the North Sea. All stages of our past are represented from prehistory, through the Roman invasions, the early medieval kingdoms, the great castles, abbeys and churches of the middle ages, towns and industry to the defence of Britain. Many buildings demonstrate Scotland's wider cultural connections within the Roman empire, the medieval Christian world or today's industrial society. As Duke of Rothesay, I am particularly pleased to see included Rothesay Castle, resplendent in its moat, and Duff House, which I had the pleasure of opening in 1995 after its refurbishment.

All the ancient monuments and historic buildings illustrated and described in this book are in the care of Historic Scotland, the Government Agency charged with the duty of caring for Scotland's built heritage, because they no longer serve their original function. Not all such buildings can be taken over by the state and Historic Scotland also plays an important role in helping to save abandoned and derelict buildings and find new uses for them. One important example is Stanley Mills near Perth, where collaboration between Historic Scotland and the Phoenix Trust is leading to the conservation of a new monument in state care and the creation of private housing and industrial workshops.

I very much welcome this action by Historic Scotland, as I welcome this book which offers a new insight into Scotland's past: her history told through her built heritage. An added bonus is that all the ancient monuments and historic buildings illustrated in this book, being in state care, are open to the public, and there to be enjoyed.

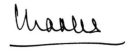

*For Pamela*

# INTRODUCTION

About ten thousand years ago, our ancestors followed the retreating ice northwards into the area we now call Scotland. They gradually spread over the whole country, living by trapping wild animals, fishing, collecting shellfish and gathering edible wild food. They lived in simple but nevertheless effective shelters formed of skins or brushwood covering a wooden framework. Stone tools were used and scatters of the debris from the manufacture of such implements have been found. It is likely that these people also used organic materials, which have not been preserved. By comparing them with other hunter-gatherers who still survive it is likely that they had a complex set of cultural and religious beliefs.

About 6000 years ago, new ideas filtered through from the east: crops could be specially grown and animals domesticated – fields came later. At about this time, people started to build major monuments in the landscape; amongst the earliest known monuments in Scotland are burial mounds made of soil and stones. Houses were still built of wood, but they were much larger and more substantial than before. In Orkney, the earliest known houses (and a workshop) were of stone, partly because there was good building stone there, but also probably because wood was scarce.

A little later, the construction of stone circles and other settings of stones is eloquent testimony to a strong religious belief. These people also understood the movement of the sun and the stars, though these observations may not have been related to detailed astronomy, but to the religious observance of the cycle of the seasons.

Houses, workshops, temples and tombs have continued to be built during the centuries which have followed: they have been joined in more recent times by roads, canals, railways and bridges. The most durable building materials have generally remained the same for millennia: stone, wood, earth, turf. Historic Scotland has in its care over 300 such monuments. These range in date from the two houses erected over 5000 years ago at the Knap of Howar in Orkney to military defence works built during World War II, a little over 50 years ago. They include a wide range of buildings of all periods and of all types from the houses of the upper echelons of society – prehistoric brochs, medieval castles, lairds' town houses – to other buildings representing ordinary people: hut circles, Norse longhouses, a Hebridean blackhouse, market crosses and a Victorian gasworks.

Together these are a significant part of the built heritage of Scotland, a sample of the tens of thousands of structures from every era that still survive in our hills and fields. They carry and contain evidence for how people lived, their architectural pretensions, their artistic and engineering skills, and their ambitions; but equally importantly they are part of the history of Scotland, providing, in one sense at least, a monumental history of the land and its people.

# A

# MONUMENTAL HISTORY

# OF SCOTLAND

A Pictish horseman carved on one of the
Aberlemno stones, eighth century (see page 41).

# S K A R A
# BRAE

In Orkney lies the most famous prehistoric village in Western Europe, Skara Brae. The village was rediscovered during a great storm in 1850. The earliest houses were built here perhaps a little before 3000 BC, though the main phase of the settlement dates to about 500 years later. In the settlement there were perhaps eight houses and a workshop linked by two passages. Each house was roughly square but with rounded corners, entered through a single doorway, and contained a stone dresser, facing the door, and two beds flanking the central hearth. The walls were up to 3m (10ft) high. The roof was probably of turf supported on rafters of timber or whalebone.

The people who lived at Skara Brae were farmers and fishers as well as hunters. They used tools of stone, bone and wood. While we do not know what they wore, they were clearly fond of jewellery, for many beads, pendants and pins have been found here.

Skara Brae appears to have been abandoned about 2500 BC, but the reason remains a mystery.

# THE STONES OF
# STENNESS

The later inhabitants of Skara Brae lived at the time the great stone circle at Stenness was erected near where the Lochs of Harray and Stenness come together. Pottery of the same type as used by the inhabitants of Skara Brae was found here.

Stone circles were used for religious ceremonies. Cattle and sheep bones in the ditch at Stenness may have resulted from feasts or sacrifices, while in the centre of the circle was a stone setting, rather like a large hearth. There is even some evidence of trance-inducing drugs being consumed on such sites from the decorated 'grooved wear' pottery of the period.

Behind the Stones of Stenness, to the west, loom the hills of the island of Hoy.

# M A E S
# HOWE

The great mound which covers Maes Howe cannot prepare the visitor for the sight of one of the most exciting architectural spaces in Europe, the central 4.6m (15ft) square chamber, nearly as high as it is long. Formed of sandstone flags, it is dry-stone built, with a corbelled roof. The visual effect is heightened by four massive upright monoliths, one at each corner.

The chamber is entered through a long passage, along which the sun shines at midwinter sunset to cast a beam of light on the entrance to the tomb at the end. To each side of the chamber is another tomb, each cell blocked by a single stone, as was the main entrance.

Maes Howe was built about 3000 BC, and is thus contemporary with Skara Brae and the Stones of Stenness. About 4000 years after its construction, Vikings broke into the tomb and carved runic messages on its walls, including 'Vemundre carved' (above).

# CALANAIS

The great stone setting at Calanais (or Callanish) in Lewis is unique in Scotland. The setting is cruciform in shape, the main arm being an avenue 80m (270ft) long. In the centre is a circle of 13 stones with a central monolith over 4m (12ft) tall, and a burial cairn. The oldest visible part of this great ceremonial site – probably the stone circle – was erected about 3000 BC and the monument continued in use until about 800 BC. The erection of the stones was not the earliest activity on the site. Excavation has demonstrated that the site had previously been ploughed.

# LOANHEAD OF
# DAVIOT

In north-east Scotland is a special group of stone circles, known as recumbent stone circles. They are so named because of the way in which they are constructed – a single large slab lies on its side between two uprights. The uprights are carefully graded down in height away from the recumbent stone which always lies on the south or south-west side of the circle. Excavations have shown that the interior of the circle at Loanhead of Daviot was heavily burnt before the low cairn was erected, perhaps as part of a ritual cleansing. This monument was probably used over several centuries within the thousand years from 3000 to 2000 BC, and perhaps even later.

# CAIRNPAPPLE

On a hill in West Lothian, commanding wide views, Cairnpapple was a religious site for over 3000 years. Before 3000 BC a temple was built, known to us as a henge; its ceremonial boundary consisted of a ditch (seen in the foreground) with an external bank. Within the henge 24 standing stones were erected: these were later removed but today their former locations are marked by a circle of pits.

Some centuries later the focus of activity changed from ritual to burial. Several burials were made inside the henge, one within a low mound (see above). That mound was later subsumed within a larger cairn and then an even larger cairn. It was to be another thousand years before there was further activity at Cairnpapple. Then, four graves were dug in the space between the cairn and the henge ditch.

After excavations in 1947 and 1948 the earlier cairn was reconstructed, with the later cairn marked as a stone platform.

# ACHNABRECK

 Among the most enigmatic prehistoric survivals are cup-and-ring marks. These marks were clearly carved for a significant purpose for they were carefully made. They might be carved on individual stones, or on great sheets of rock, as here at Achnabreck in Argyll. They might be simple or complex, again as here where some designs have many concentric rings while lines connect separate rings. Recent research has shown that many examples of such rock art are situated at good viewing points and on routes between lowland and upland summer pasture.

# THE BROCH OF
# GURNESS

Brochs are large round houses, dry-stone built and dating to the centuries around the birth of Christ. Over 500 are known, mainly in the north and north-west of Scotland. Their thick walls and lack of external openings – apart from a securely defended door – suggest that they were erected at least partly for defence, though display, or at least prestige, may have played a part. The broch at Gurness in Orkney sits within its own enclosure, and round its base, within the defences, clusters a village of stone-built houses. Perhaps the broch was the house of the local chief.

Brochs often contain a well or water tank and a hearth. A scarcement or ledge at first-floor level indicates the possibility of a second floor, or an internal roof. Stairs in the thickness of the wall led to the top of the broch.

# MOUSA

Today, only a handful of brochs stands to an appreciable height: Mousa is the most striking. Situated on an uninhabited island in Shetland, it withstood siege during Viking times yet still stands 13m (43ft) high.

# ARDESTIE
## SOUTERRAIN

Next to the foundations of a row of four round houses at Ardestie, near Dundee, is an underground passage. Termed souterrains in Scotland, these passages are found in France, Ireland and Cornwall as well as Scotland, where they are widespread, and appear to date to the Iron Age. Usually, the underground passage was entered from a house, suggesting that it served as a storage cellar. Other uses which have been suggested include refuge and religious ceremonies. Ardestie seems to have been used for storage then deliberately infilled about the end of the second century AD.

# GRAIN
## SOUTERRAIN

The souterrain at Grain in Orkney survives with its roof intact, supported on stone pillars.

# E D I N ' S
# HALL

Sitting on the shoulder of a hill in the Scottish Borders is the settlement known as Edin's Hall. It lies within a defensive enclosure. Such forts first appear in Scotland about 1000 BC. Thus the surrounding enclosure was probably old when the broch was built, around the second century AD.

In floor area, the broch (above left) is the largest known, yet, unlike Mousa, it probably did not stand high. It is one of the few brochs which were constructed outside their main area of concentration in the north of Scotland. At Edin's Hall we can also see evidence for another trend: the abandonment of the defences and the spread of houses over them (above right). This is quite common in the Borders and may hint at an increasing population. The abandonment of defended enclosures may also be one of the results of the imposition of the *pax Romana* in the north.

# HOLYROOD
# PARK

Prehistoric archaeological remains can survive in surprising places. These cultivation terraces lie in Holyrood Park in the centre of Edinburgh. A farmstead of Iron-Age type lies nearby and it is probable that the terraced fields were part of this farm occupied about 2000 years ago.

In the foreground is Dunsapie Loch. This is a modern creation. The present-day look of the Royal Park of Holyrood owes much to the work and inspiration of Prince Albert, husband of Queen Victoria.

# THE ANTONINE
# WALL

Scotland lay on the north-west frontier of the Roman empire and it is thus appropriate that the surviving Roman monuments of the period are all military in nature. They include the earthwork remains of temporary camps, frontiers, forts, fortlets, towers and roads. All bear witness to the activities of one of the greatest armies which the world has ever seen. This army brought southern and eastern Scotland into the Roman empire on three occasions, from AD 79 to about 87, from 142 to about 163 and from 208 to 211. After that date, the Romans were content to maintain surveillance over southern Scotland from Hadrian's Wall and its outpost forts.

The foremost Roman military monument in Scotland is the Antonine Wall. Built in the years following 142 by the army on the orders of the Emperor Antoninus Pius, it stretched for 40 Roman miles from modern Bo'ness on the Forth to Old Kilpatrick on the Clyde. It consisted of a rampart of turf, placed on a stone base 15 Roman feet (4.3m) wide, and probably topped by a timber breastwork. In front lay a wide and deep ditch: the best surviving stretch is at Watling Lodge in Falkirk (left). Forts lay at roughly 2-mile intervals along the Wall, connected by a road, the Military Way. Between some pairs of forts lay a fortlet. The Antonine Wall is believed to have been abandoned in about 163.

# BEARSDEN
## BATH-HOUSE

Generally, each fort was provided with a bath-house, on the Antonine Wall often placed in an annexe. That at Bearsden was discovered during excavations in 1973.

The bath-house, which was provided for the use of all the soldiers in the fort, offered two forms of bathing: the steam treatment (a Turkish bath) and the hot, dry heat or sauna.

Along the main spine of the bath-house lay a changing-room to the right, marked out by short timber posts; the cold room with, to this side, the hot dry room and, beyond, the cold bath; and the three rooms of the steam range – two warm rooms and the hot room with the hot bath beyond. At top left, behind the bath-house, the latrines completed the sanitary arrangements.

# DUMBARTON ROCK

One of the longest-occupied fortified sites in Britain, the characteristic twin-peaked profile of Dumbarton Rock is a familiar sight to travellers along the Clyde. In the fifth century the Rock became the capital of a kingdom, Strathclyde, which was to last over 500 years. It was to the Christian Coroticus, King of Strathclyde, that St Patrick wrote in about 450 to demand the return of some of his converts who had been captured and forced into slavery.

In the Middle Ages, Dumbarton was a royal castle and until the Battle of Largs in 1263 was a bulwark against Norse invasion of the Scottish kingdom. Mary Queen of Scots sailed from here to France in 1548 to marry the Dauphin Francis, and the castle held out for her after she fled to England in 1568.

In 1735 the castle was rebuilt as one of the Government's strongholds along the edge of the Highlands and most of the surviving buildings date to that time.

PE RIAPV
ST OH

# WHITHORN

At an unknown date, perhaps in the fifth century, St Ninian established a mission at Whithorn in Galloway and built a church, dedicated to St Martin of Tours, which was called Candida Casa, the white house. Although his church has not survived, several Christian stones found at Whithorn and nearby Kirkmadrine date to the early Middle Ages. One of the earliest is the 'Peter' stone, found beside the road south to the Isle of Whithorn It records that this was the place of Peter the Apostle: the place was presumably holy ground. The style of lettering suggests that it was erected in the seventh century.

St Ninian's monastery became a famous seat of learning and his shrine a famous place of pilgrimage for penitents from England and Ireland as well as Scotland. Robert the Bruce came here shortly before his death in 1329: his enemy Edward II had visited in 1302 while still Prince of Wales. Recent excavations have thrown further light on the Norse and medieval history of the site.

# DUNADD

In about 500 the Scotti from Ireland, first recorded by the Romans in 360 as raiders, conquered Argyll. Here they created their own kingdom which they called Dalriada. One of their capitals lay at Dunadd. On the top of the hill a footprint cut into the rock may have been used in the inauguration ceremony of their kings. Several other similar footprints are known elsewhere in Scotland, while a shoe or slipper featured in the inauguration ceremony of the Irish kings.

Artefacts found here demonstrate contacts with other northern kingdoms, the Picts and the Angles of Northumbria. Dalriadan kings also married into the Pictish royal family; thus, in about 843, their king, Kenneth MacAlpin, succeeded to that kingdom too. He moved his capital to Pictland: Dunadd was abandoned, but the name of the Scots triumphed.

# EILEACH AN NAIOMH

St Columba, born in Ireland, founded the Christian church in Dalriada and died at his monastery on Iona in 597. His disciples established other monasteries in Scotland.

The desire to follow the contemplative life formed a strong strand of early Christianity. Some withdrew from society altogether. On one of the Garvellach islands, south of Mull, a beehive cell of such a hermit survives. The Life of St Brendan of Clonfert, better known as 'the Voyager', states that he established a church on the island of Ailech where he intended to spend the rest of his days, but in the event he returned to Ireland. Ailech has traditionally been identified as Eileach an Naiomh.

The cell on Eieach an Naiomh consists of two inter-connecting rooms, each with a corbelled roof. Elsewhere, caves might be used for the same purpose.

Although St Columba's followers converted the Picts and the Angles of Northumbria, it was at Whitby in Northumbria in 663 that the death knell of Columban Christianity was sounded when the Roman calendar was preferred to the Columban. In time, all Scotland gave allegiance to the Roman church.

# PICTISHSYMBOL
# STONES

The Picts enter history in 297 when they were first mentioned by a Roman writer. However, they were not newcomers to Scotland, but were the descendants of the Caledonians and other tribes recorded earlier. It was perhaps another 300 years before we see the full flowering of their art: by that time their kingdom encompassed all the land north of the Forth-Clyde isthmus with the exception of Argyll.

The earliest symbols were carved on undressed stones. Those on the earliest stone at Aberlemno in Angus (above) are a serpent, Z-rod, double disc, mirror and comb. The last four symbols appear in pairs, as occurs on many stones.

The adoption of Christianity brought a major change – the appearance of crosses and biblical scenes on stones. The front face of the Eassie stone (left) is dominated by the cross but other figures appear in the corners, including a foot soldier (bottom left of picture).

# ST ANDREWS
## SARCOPHAGUS

In 1833, during gravedigging, part of a sarcophagus was found in the space between St Andrews Cathedral and St Rule's Tower. Dating to about 800, this probably held the remains of an important saint or king. The main panel of the sarcophagus is devoted to scenes from the life of King David of Israel. The main figure is of David fighting the lion.

This is one of the finest carvings to have survived from early medieval Europe. Together with other sculpture it emphasizes the importance of the Bishop of St Andrews, the leading churchman in medieval Scotland.

# KILDALTON
## HIGH CROSS

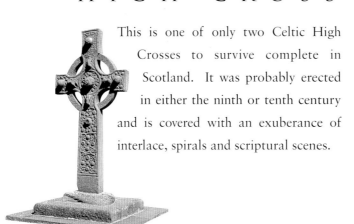

This is one of only two Celtic High Crosses to survive complete in Scotland. It was probably erected in either the ninth or tenth century and is covered with an exuberance of interlace, spirals and scriptural scenes.

# R U T H W E L L
# CROSS

The Angles landed on the east coast of north England and south Scotland in the sixth century and over the next three centuries extended their hold over the land southwards to the Humber-Mersey line and northwards to the Forth – and beyond. In 731 they established their own bishopric at Whithorn.

Perhaps 50 or more years earlier, this great cross had been erected at Ruthwell on the north shore of the Solway. It was probably a preaching cross. All four faces of the cross are carved, but only the two main faces with figures, which are both religious and secular. The south face includes a depiction of Christ in glory. The cross bears inscriptions in both Latin and runes, including an extract from the poem *The Vision of the Cross*.

# JARLSHOF

In 793 the monks of the island of Lindisfarne in Northumbria witnessed a new and terrible scourge – a Viking raid. In time these raiders from Norway came to settle as well as plunder. One of their settlements lay at what is now called Jarlshof, by the southern tip of Shetland, where it was built on a site stretching back to the Bronze Age. (The photograph above shows boats under sail scratched on stones found at Jarlshof.) The main type of dwelling was the longhouse, whose late descendant is the Arnol blackhouse (see page 115).

Shetland formed part of the Norse earldom of Orkney. These Earls owned land in Norway as well as Scotland and might as easily be buried in Bergen or Trondheim as in Orkney. The last Norse Earl died in 1231, and his successors were generally Scots, owing obedience to the Kings of Scots as well as the Kings of Norway. Yet it was not until 1468/9 that Orkney and Shetland came into the kingdom of Scotland: the islands were Norse or Norwegian longer than they have been Scottish! Jarlshof is not a genuine name, but the exotic invention of Sir Walter Scott in his novel *The Pirate*.

# DUNFERMLINE
# ABBEY

The reign of Malcolm III Canmore (1058–93) marked a watershed in Scottish history. He and his queen, Margaret, a princess of the English royal line, established a new form of succession to the throne, finally overturning the Pictish traditions of alternating lines of succession within the royal family and, as if to mark that change, built a new family mausoleum at Dunfermline in Fife, abandoning the centuries-old tradition of royal burial at Iona.

Dunfermline was almost certainly the first monastery of the Benedictine order to be established in Scotland. The original monastery does not survive for it was rebuilt by David I, son of Malcolm and Margaret, in 1128. Only the nave of David's church survives today, bearing eloquent witness to its construction by the masons who had earlier worked on Durham Cathedral.

Dunfermline was to retain its importance until James VI moved south in 1603. Generations of the royal family, including Robert the Bruce, were buried here and later a palace was built next to the monastery, the ruins of which still survive. Here Charles I was born in 1600.

# JEDBURGH
# ABBEY

The imposing south face of Jedburgh Abbey is the first ancient monument seen by many visitors to Scotland. Founded about 1138, it was one of the many monasteries established by David I. David erected his monastery on an earlier Christian site, which was probably that founded by Bishop Ecgred of Lindisfarne in 830, though sculpture dating to the previous century suggests that there was an even older Christian church here.

Jedburgh at the time of Bishop Ecgred lay within the Anglian kingdom of Northumbria. One of the most famous sons of the area was St Cuthbert. A shepherd on the Lammermuir Hills, he had entered the monastery at Old Melrose following a vision. In time he became Prior of Old Melrose and then Prior of Lindisfarne in 664. During the Viking raids, monks of Lindisfarne carried his body to Old Melrose for safety. After further travels they eventually settled at Durham where they erected a cathedral over St Cuthbert's final resting place.

# DUFFUS
# CASTLE

It was in the reigns of Malcolm III (1058–93) and his son David I (1124–53) that most Flemings and Normans are known to have settled in Scotland. The incomers brought with them feudalism and the castle. The motte (mound) and bailey castle was the main instrument of their domination and they built those wherever they settled to help maintain their control. One fine example of such a castle is Duffus.

The great motte of Duffus was built by Freskin, a Flemish soldier who had been granted lands in Moray by David I, about 1150. A timber castle would have sat on the top: the present stone keep dates to about 200 years later.

Freskin was the ancestor of the Moray and Murray families, whose ranks include the Morays of Bothwell, the Dukes of Atholl, the Earls of Dunmore, Dysart, Mansfield and Tullibardine and the Barons Nairne. It was a Lady Nairne who wrote the famous Jacobite song 'Charlie is my darling'.

# ROTHESAY CASTLE

For several centuries the Hebrides were held by the Norse. Bute was one of the first islands to be reclaimed by the Scottish Crown. In about 1200 William I (1165–1214) granted it to Alan his steward, ancestor of the Stewart kings of Scotland. The castle has been held by the family ever since, and today its hereditary keeper is the Marquess of Bute, a direct descendant of King Robert II.

Rothesay is the only circular castle – as opposed to tower – in Scotland. Its defensive wall was probably erected by 1230 when the castle was besieged and captured by Uspak King of Man and the Isles. Although it soon returned to Scots hands, it was recaptured in 1263 by King Hakon IV of Norway. By the Treaty of Perth in 1266 it finally returned to the Scottish kingdom.

The Stewart kings remained interested in Rothesay Castle, repairing and strengthening it over several centuries, and granting the title Duke of Rothesay to the monarch's eldest son: Prince Charles' principal Scottish title is Duke of Rothesay.

# BOTHWELL CASTLE

The death of the Maid of Norway, granddaughter of Alexander III (1249–86), in 1290 resulted in a succession crisis. The two main claimants to the throne were John Balliol and Robert Bruce, After hearing all the rival claimants or 'Competitors', King Edward I of England decided in favour of Balliol in 1292. His reign lasted less than four years before he was deposed by Edward, who then tried to rule the country directly. But Scotland would not accept alien rule and ten years later, in 1306, Robert the Bruce, grandson of the 'Competitor' of 1292 had himself crowned King at Scone. The independence of Scotland was assured by the Battle of Bannockburn in 1314.

The Wars of Independence saw the fall of many families and the rise of new – and the fall of many castles and, eventually, the building of new. The Moray family of Bothwell (descendants of Freskin: see page 52) was a telling example of both. Sir Andrew Moray, with William Wallace, was the victor of the Battle of Stirling Bridge in 1297, but he died soon after, probably of wounds sustained in the fight. His father and both his grandsons died in English prisons; the family extinguished itself in service to the Crown.

The Morays' principal castle was Bothwell. It was besieged in 1301 by Edward I, falling to him in less than a month, and again in 1336 when it was captured by Edward III. The following year it was recaptured by Sir Andrew Moray who then partly demolished the donjon to render the castle useless.

# DUNSTAFFNAGE
# CASTLE

Few early stone medieval castles survive on mainland Scotland. This is because Robert the Bruce ordered their destruction to prevent them being used by the English. Early castles do survive, however, in western Scotland, an area largely outside the range of English armies. One such stronghold is Dunstaffnage Castle at the mouth of Loch Etive.

Perched spectacularly on a rock, Dunstaffnage was built in the middle of the thirteenth century by the MacDougalls. It was captured by Robert the Bruce in 1309 and retained in royal hands until 1470, when it was granted to the Campbells who shortly afterwards erected the gatehouse tower. Dunstaffnage has remained a Campbell castle ever since. In 1746 Flora MacDonald was briefly imprisoned here following the Battle of Culloden and the escape of Prince Charles Edward Stuart.

# KILMARTIN

Some of the best depictions of medieval warriors can be found in western Scotland. These stones at Kilmartin in Argyll are fine examples of the flowering of West Highland sculpture in the fourteenth and fifteenth centuries, when the Hebrides formed part of the Lordship of the Isles. One of the titles held by Prince Charles is that of Lord of the Isles.

# CAERLAVEROCK
# CASTLE

The lands of Caerlaverock were granted to the Maxwells about 1220 and are still in the hands of their descendants. Tree-ring dating of the timbers of the first bridge over the moat demonstrates that the castle was built about 1277. In 1300 it was besieged by Edward I of England with an army of 87 knights and 3000 men, and soon captured.

Caerlaverock was repaired in the 1330s and became one of the major strongholds of the Western Marches. The courtyard accommodation was modernized in the 1630s by Robert Maxwell, first Earl of Nithsdale, in a fashionable Renaissance style. Like most of his line, he was a strong supporter of the Crown and during the troubles of 1640 held Caerlaverock for King Charles I. A siege of 13 weeks ended in capture by the Covenanters and partial dismantling of the castle which was never re-occupied.

# GLASGOW
## CATHEDRAL

The most complete medieval cathedral surviving on the Scottish mainland, Glasgow Cathedral was also the shrine of St Kentigern, sometimes known as St Mungo. The cathedral was mostly built over a period of 150 years from about 1240 and was specially designed to allow pilgrims to the shrine to progress round the building. The lofty stone spire, erected about 1400, is a local landmark.

The Bishops of Glasgow were amongst the most important men of the kingdom. Bishop Wishart was one of Robert the Bruce's strongest supporters and produced from his treasury the robes in which the king was enthroned at Scone in 1306.

After the Reformation in 1560 the cathedral was divided into three parish churches, but was restored to one in the nineteenth century. It is still in use today.

# THE TOMB OF
# SIR JAMES DOUGLAS

The Wars of Independence produced some great Scottish heroes. Ranking immediately after Wallace and Bruce stands 'The Good' Sir James Douglas. One of Bruce's staunchest supporters, in 1330 he carried the heart of the dead King on Crusade. Sir James died in battle against the Moors in Spain. The heart was brought back to Scotland and buried at Melrose Abbey in accordance with Bruce's wishes. Sir James was buried at the family mausoleum, St Bride's Church at Douglas, where several of his successors were also interred.

# THREAVE
# CASTLE

The Douglases were one of Scotland's great baronial families. The main line, the 'Black' Douglases, were descendants of 'The Good' Sir James (see page 64). The Black Douglases held extensive estates in Scotland, including Bothwell Castle (see page 56). The main stronghold in Galloway of Archibald 'the Grim', third Earl of Douglas, and head of the Black Douglas line, lay on the island of Threave in the Galloway Dee. The great tower was built between 1369 and 1400 and the outer wall in about 1450. In spite of its appearance of strength, the castle fell to James II in 1455 – though only by trickery, not by force – and the power of the Black Douglases was broken from that day.

# TANTALLON
# CASTLE

Although the 'Black' Douglas line came to an end in 1455, the junior line, the 'Red' Douglases, have continued to this day, the head of the family being the Duke of Hamilton. Tantallon in East Lothian was the principal seat of the Red Douglases. Its great curtain wall was probably erected by William, first Earl of Douglas, between 1358 and his death in 1384.

The curtain wall, nearly 4m (10ft) thick, has suffered bombardment by cannon, being repaired, heightened and modernized on various occasions. It stands today as a powerful symbol of the power and ambition of medieval barons.

# SMAILHOLM
# TOWER

Smailholm, standing on its rocky pinnacle, is often seen as the archetypal Scottish tower house. It was built in the fifteenth century by the Pringles, squires to the Earls of Douglas, and was basically a strongly fortified farmhouse of a type found on both sides of the border. In the early seventeenth century Smailholm was bought by Sir William Scott of Harden. It was to Smailholm, where his grandfather farmed, that Walter Scott came as a sickly child in the 1770s to recover his health. Thus was created in the later Sir Walter his love of the lore and legend of the Borders which infused so much of his poetry and prose.

Scott not only invented the historical novel, but he also changed people's perception of the countryside. Previously it had been seen as barren, but he brought people to appreciate it for its own qualities. His own enthusiasm for the region engendered similar feelings in others and so painters such as Girton and Turner came north to immortalize the Scottish Borders on canvas. Scott is buried at Dryburgh Abbey.

# TORPHICHEN PRECEPTORY

In the Middle Ages the Church in Scotland was part of an international community. There were links not only with Rome, but with monasteries in Western Europe and, through the military orders, with the Eastern Mediterranean. A surviving expression of the latter is the church of the Knights of St John, often known as the Hospitallers, at Torphichen in West Lothian. The surviving tower and transepts were erected in the fifteenth century in a castellated style.

# TULLIBARDINE CHAPEL

In the fifteenth century many lairds established chapels where prayers could be said in perpetuity for the souls of the founder and his family. The colleges of priests who celebrated mass gave their name to such churches – collegiate chapels.

Tullibardine Chapel was founded by Sir David Murray in 1446. Descendant of Freskin of Moray (see page 52), he was an ancestor of the Dukes of Atholl.

# THE ABBOT'S HOUSE,
# ARBROATH

Monasteries in Scotland continued to develop right up to the Reformation. Some of the changes marked departures from earlier regulations of the Order. Abbots often no longer lived with their monks, but in their own houses. One such establishment was at Arbroath Abbey, founded in 1176 by King William the Lion, who was buried in the church. It was from the abbey that the famous Declaration of Arbroath was issued in 1320.

# CROSSRAGUEL
# ABBEY

The Kennedy family came to have close links with Crossraguel Abbey in the sixteenth century. Kennedy abbots undertook major building works at the abbey, to the church and to the accommodation. A tower house was built for the abbot in about 1530. At the same time, this gatehouse was erected to provide an impressive entrance to his new residence. Although the abbey had long been defined by a precinct wall, the new gatehouse – and tower – were further embellished with gun-loops, the whole adding up to a sternly fortified dwelling.

# EDINBURGH CASTLE

Edinburgh's castle still dominates the city as it has done for centuries. Over 3000 years ago people first settled here. Their successors watched the Romans come and go. From Edinburgh, King Mynyddog set out in about 570 with 300 men to fight and die against the Angles at the Battle of Catraeth (Catterick). By 1093 a royal castle had been established on the rock and here died Queen – later Saint – Margaret who is still commemorated in the chapel which bears her name. Within the walls of the castle lies one of Scotland's royal palaces, which served not only as the home of kings but the storehouse for their records and regalia. It was for the better protection of the Honours of Scotland (the Crown jewels) that James VI of Scotland and I of England, himself born in the castle in 1566, created the Crown Room in 1617.

# THE HONOURS OF SCOTLAND AND THE STONE OF DESTINY

'No king was ever wont to reign in Scotland unless he had first sat upon this stone at Scone'. The Stone was taken from Scone Abbey by Edward I of England in 1296 and given to Westminster Abbey where it sat in the Coronation Chair for nearly 700 years. In 1996 the Stone was returned to Scotland: it now rests in the Crown Room in Edinburgh Castle with the Honours of Scotland.

The crown was made for James V and first used at the coronation of Mary Queen of Scots at Stirling in 1543. James IV received the sceptre from Pope Alexander VI in 1494 and the sword from Pope Julius II in 1507. Together these three magnificent objects form the Honours of Scotland, the oldest set of Crown jewels in Britain and amongst the oldest in Europe.

# S T I R L I N G
# CASTLE

The Stewart kings specially favoured Stirling as a residence. James IV built the Great Hall and the royal residence known as the King's Old Building, James V the Palace and James VI the Chapel Royal. The Palace was erected in the years following 1538. Here the young Mary Queen of Scots spent much of her life until her departure for France in 1548.

The Palace is the most accomplished Renaissance building in Scotland. James V had visited France and both his wives were French. It is thus not surprising that he brought over French masons to help create his masterpiece.

There are indications that the interior was also sumptuously furnished. The ceiling of one of the rooms of the King's Apartment was decorated with wooden roundels, the Stirling Heads. It is not possible to identify most of the characters displayed on the plaques, though some are thought to represent the Royal family and members of the Court.

# S T I R L I N G
# BRIDGE

Roads were poor in Scotland in the Middle Ages. It is not surprising that Mary Queen of Scots was said to possess the only carriage in the country at the time. But many places which now seem remote were then accessible by sea. Ferries allowed travellers to cross rivers and some rivers were bridged. The Old Bridge at Stirling has survived since that time, though one arch was replaced in 1749 after it had been blown up in 1745 to prevent the Jacobite army entering the town. It remained the lowest crossing point on the Forth until Kincardine Bridge was erected in 1936.

# ST ANDREWS
# CASTLE

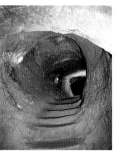

The castle at St Andrews was the home of the Bishop, later Archbishop, of St Andrews. Founded about 1200, it was rebuilt on several occasions. The final work was undertaken by Archbishop Hamilton following the great siege of 1546–7, one of the most famous of the events leading up to the Reformation.

In 1546 Cardinal David Beaton, Archbishop of St Andrews, burnt the Protestant preacher George Wishart in front of the castle for heresy. Two months later the castle was seized by a group of local Protestants who murdered the Cardinal and hung his body from a window of his own stronghold. The Protestants in turn were besieged by the Regent, the Earl of Arran, acting on behalf of the infant Mary Queen of Scots. Unable to capture the castle, the besiegers started digging a mine intended to go under the ditch and give access to the courtyard (above). However, their work was detected by the Protestants who started their own counter-mine, eventually successfully breaking through. Notwithstanding this failure, Arran captured the castle – with help from a French fleet – and the Protestants, including John Knox, were condemned to the galleys or imprisoned. In 1554 Arran was replaced as Regent by Mary of Guise, mother of Mary Queen of Scots. Following her death in 1560, Parliament passed a law changing the religion of the country to Protestantism.

# HERMITAGE CASTLE

Hermitage, in Liddesdale, is one of the great Border strongholds. Although the oldest part was built by the English Sir Hugh de Dacre, it was acquired by William, first Earl of Douglas, in 1371 and remained in the hands of that family until 1492 when Archibald Douglas, fifth Earl of Angus, was forced to exchange Hermitage for Bothwell Castle (see page 56).

Hermitage thus came into the hands of Patrick Hepburn, first Earl of Bothwell. His descendant, James, fourth Earl, was the third husband of Mary Queen of Scots. In 1566, before the marriage, the Queen gave Bothwell a special commission to enforce royal authority in the Borders. Bothwell, injured in an affray, was visited on 16 October by the Queen who rode the 50 miles to and from Jedburgh in the day. Bothwell almost certainly was behind the plot to murder the Queen's husband, Darnley, on 10 February 1567. Mary's subsequent marriage to Bothwell united their enemies and led to Mary's imprisonment in Lochleven Castle and Bothwell's flight to Norway where he was captured: Bothwell died a prisoner in Denmark in 1578.

Lost to the Bothwells in 1594, the castle also lost its purpose in 1603 when King James VI succeeded to the throne of England. The castle owes much of its appearance today to the fifth Duke of Buccleuch who ordered its repair in the early nineteenth century.

# E D Z E L L
# CASTLE

Gardens were an important adjunct to major castles from at least the fifteenth century, offering food as well as relaxation. Rich landowners kept up with the latest fashion, re-designing their gardens as necessary. One of the finest gardens was designed for Sir David Lindsay at Edzell in 1604 (the present garden was restored in the 1930s). The garden contained many heraldic and symbolic devices, enhanced by the flowers which reflected the colours in the Lindsay coat-of-arms. The box hedge spelled out the family motto DUM SPIRO SPERO, 'while I breathe I hope'.

The tower house, built of the distinctive local red sandstone, was erected in the early sixteenth century. Later that century, Mary Queen of Scots stayed at Edzell and on 25 August 1562 held a meeting of the Privy Council in the castle.

# K I N N E I L
# H O U S E
# B O ' N E S S

Too often, historic buildings only survive as bare walls, shorn of their decoration. At the palace built in the 1540s and 1550s at Kinneil by James Hamilton, second Earl of Arran and Regent for the infant Mary Queen of Scots, however, some magnificent wall paintings remain. The Parable of the Good Samaritan is one of several biblical scenes and probably dates to 1553–4.

This man the leuite be...
the law of nature qualis...do the...
this preste pe...law of...
...

# ST ANDREWS, WEST PORT

It was under King David I (1125–53) that the first royal burghs were established. In time, some came to be protected by walls. Rarely do these walls survive in Scotland; however, some gates exist. One example is at St Andrews. The building contract for the gate is dated 18 May 1589. The entrance was flanked by towers and protected by gun-loops. The gate was renovated in 1843 when the arms over the road were replaced by the present sculpture.

# PRESTON MARKET CROSS

An important feature of the burgh was the market cross. At Preston in East Lothian is the only market cross of its type which still stands where it was erected, probably soon after 1617. The shaft is surmounted by a unicorn. The parapet would have been used for announcements and the vaulted chamber beneath as a gaol.

# A R G Y L L ' S
# LODGING

The aristocracy often built houses in towns such as Edinburgh and Stirling so as to be near their monarch. Argyll's Lodging was largely erected by the Earl of Stirling about 1630 after the court had moved to London. Twenty-five years later the house was bought and extended by the ninth Earl of Argyll, whose other great Lowland residence lay nearby at Castle Campbell.

In the eighteenth century, when the adjacent Stirling Castle was an army barracks the house became a military hospital. During the 1960s, it did further duty as a youth hostel. It was finally opened to the public by Historic Scotland in 1997; the extensive refurbishments were completed using information gleaned from an original inventory.

# SKELMORLIE
# AISLE

 Nobles and lairds often made advance provision for their burial. At Largs in 1636, Sir Robert Montgomerie of Skelmorlie erected a spendid tomb, unique in Scotland. The burial vault sits within an aisle containing the laird's loft and with a richly painted timber barrel-vaulted roof.

The tomb is in the Renaissance style, but was probably made by Scottish masons using foreign pattern books. The decoration included the arms of Sir Robert and his wife, Dame Margaret Douglas: their coffins still rest in the vault below the tomb.

The ceiling, dated 1638, was the work of J S Stalker, who had earlier served his apprenticeship at Edinburgh Castle. Prominent in the decoration again are the arms of Sir Robert and his wife, accompanied by those of his ancestors, with biblical scenes, quotations and representations of the four seasons.

# KILCHURN CASTLE

The flight of James VII and II and the *coup d'état* of 1688 produced new governments in London and Edinburgh and opposition to both, which continued for many years. The supporters of the exiled Stuart king became known as Jacobites from the Latin for James, Jacobus.

One of Scotland's most spectacular castles, Kilchurn lies at the head of Loch Awe, on a strategic line of access through the Highlands. The castle was built by Sir Colin Campbell, first laird of Glenorchy and ancestor of the Earls and Marquesses of Breadalbane, during the years 1432 to 1475. His castle probably consisted of a tower with an attached courtyard. Various additions followed, the most notable being the conversion of the castle into a barracks for the private army of John Campbell, first Earl of Breadalbane, in the 1690s: Kilchurn is probably the oldest surviving barrack-block on the British mainland.

Although at heart a Jacobite, the Earl of Breadalbane took money from King William in order to help win over the clan chiefs. The barracks, however, were probably erected not so much to support the new dynasty as to protect the Earl's lands from his personal enemies. The castle's importance continued and it was garrisoned by the government during the Jacobite uprisings of 1715 and 1745/6 though abandoned soon after.

The Breadalbanes are no more, but Kilchurn still stands as an evocative reminder of their former power.

# DUFF
# HOUSE

The unsettled conditions of certain parts of Scotland in the eighteenth century provided opportunities for some men to make considerable sums of money. Such a man was William Duff, later first Earl Fife, who gained his wealth from selling land bonds. In 1735, Duff commissioned the architect William Adam to design a great mansion which would serve not only to demonstrate that he had 'arrived', but also to act as the capital of the great estate he had built up in the Highlands. The project collapsed amidst recrimination and a lawsuit between architect and patron in 1747 and the wings were not built. The richly ornamented centre block, however, is one of the finest Georgian baroque houses in Britain.

The Duke of Fife gave Duff House to the towns of Banff and Macduff in 1906. After a variety of uses and a period of dereliction, it re-opened in 1995 as a country house gallery.

# FORT
## GEORGE

Following the failure of the last Jacobite Uprising at the Battle of Culloden on 16 April 1746, the government renewed its attempts to control the Highlands through the strategic emplacement of garrisons at forts in the Great Glen, all linked by roads to bases in the Lowlands (see Dumbarton Rock on page 32).

The original Fort George in Inverness was destroyed by the Jacobites in 1746. After Culloden, the government sought a new base in the area and chose a promontory sticking into the Moray Firth. Here, over the years from 1748 to 1769, was erected one of the most sophisticated fortifications in Europe. Ironically, Fort George has never seen a shot fired in anger and, as a result, it survives largely unchanged.

# CORGARFF
# CASTLE

The government sometimes made use of existing tower houses as garrison posts. One such re-used tower lay at Corgarff. Here Margaret Forbes and her family had been burnt alive by the Gordons in 1571 in a particularly gruesome event during the feud between the two families.

In 1748 the government re-modelled the accommodation, erected a star-shaped wall around it, and garrisoned it with 60 men charged to maintain order and communications in the area. Corgarff continued in use into the nineteenth century when its garrison's function was to prevent smuggling.

# NEW ABBEY
# CORN MILL

In New Abbey stands a corn mill which dates to the eighteenth century but was probably built on the site of the mill built by the monks of the adjacent Sweetheart Abbey, also in Historic Scotland's care. Water was brought to the mill pond behind the mill from Loch Kindar along a lade. The water-wheel turned the great mill stones which ground the corn for the farmers of the parish.

The mill closed soon after 1945. It was restored by Charles Stewart of Shambellie in the 1970s and gifted to Historic Scotland in 1978.

# CLICK MILL DOUNBY

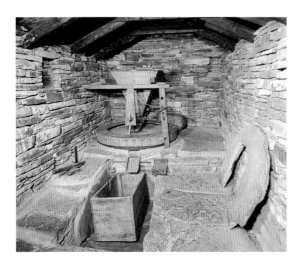

In the Northern Isles are several examples of the 'Norse' horizontal water mill, though this one, like most in Orkney, was built in the early nineteenth century. It name comes from the click caused by the knocking of the peg projecting from the upper millstone on the grain-spout which fed the grain between the stones.

# WESTQUARTER
# DOVECOT

Pigeons were often kept to supplement the diet. Many 'doocots' can still be seen in the Scottish countryside. One fine example survives at Westquarter, erected in 1647 by Sir William Livingstone of Westquarter, a relation of the Livingstones of Callander House in Falkirk. His coat of arms still sits above the entrance. The interior of the doocot is full of nesting boxes. A projecting string-course prevented animals from climbing the walls and gaining access through the openings provided for the birds.

# BONAWE IRON FURNACE

Early factories and industrial buildings were generally located in relation to the resources they needed. In the case of Bonawe Iron Furnace, the resource which drew the industry to Argyll was the abundant woodlands which could be used to make the charcoal which fired the furnace, while water from the River Awe could be tapped to drive the machinery. The site was placed on the shore of Loch Etive so as to facilitate the import of iron ore and the export of pig-iron by sea.

The ironworks were built here in 1752–53 by a group of Cumbrian ironmasters encouraged by the local laird, Sir Duncan Campbell of Lochnell. The furnace made cast-iron pigs for the use of forges in England and Wales. At its height the furnace produced 600–700 tons of pig-iron a year, an average of almost 2 tons a day. Iron production ceased at Bonawe in 1876.

The name and date of foundation of the ironworks appear on the lintel over the furnace.

# NEW LANARK
# SCHOOL

The cotton mills at New Lanark were erected beside the River Clyde in order to use the power created by the nearby Falls of Clyde. The mills and the accompanying village were founded by Robert Arkwright and David Dale in the 1780s and developed after 1785 by David Dale alone. In his care for his workforce Dale was ahead of his time, but his son-in-law Robert Owen (1771–1858) is more well known in this field through his writings.

In 1799 New Lanark was the largest cotton mill in Scotland and it was in that year that it was bought by Robert Owen. Owen continued to develop the mills and the village. He built the nursery in 1809, the shop in 1810, 'the institute for the formation of character' for adult education in 1816 and a new school (funded by profits from the shop) in the following year: the 3-storey school lies in the middle to the right of this view. Owen sold New Lanark in 1825. The mills themselves continued in production until 1968 when they were finally closed.

# K I N N A I R D
# H E A D

Scotland's coast has always been dangerous for sailors, as many wrecks testify. The Northern Lighthouse Board was established in 1786 and in the following year placed its first lighthouse on Kinnaird Head at Fraserburgh. The light was actually placed on the former castle of the Frasers and was the only time that the Board adapted an existing building. The lighthouse was built and modified by successive generations of the Stevenson family, whose most famous member was the writer Robert Louis Stevenson. It was last used on 20 June 1990, when it was replaced by an automatic light. The lighthouse is now presented in association with the adjacent lighthouse museum.

# THE BRIDGE OF
# OICH

One of the few remaining suspension bridges
suriving in Scotland, this was erected in 1850
across the Caledonian Canal.

# ARNOL
## BLACKHOUSE

The Hebridean blackhouse is the last of a line of 'longhouses' which can be traced back 1000 years to the time of the Viking invaders. This example was built in the 1860s.

The form of construction is well adapted to the local climate. The thick, low walls are dry-stone built with an earth core, the windows are small and the thatched roof displays a low pitch. Inside, most of the rooms are arranged in a row. The box beds lie at one end of the living room, to the left of the entrance; to the right is the byre, with a drain at the low end of the structure. The cattle helped to warm the house which was heated by a peat fire. There was no chimney and the nitrogen-rich thatch was regularly removed and used to fertilize the fields. Behind the house and byre lay a barn, attached to the main building, which could be accessed through a common wall in bad weather.

# BIGGAR
## GASWORKS

The gasworks at Biggar, closed in 1973, is one of the last surviving examples of a small Victorian town gasworks in Britain. It comprises a group of single-storey buildings accompanied by two gas-holders. In this reconstruction the gas man/stoker sits to have his lunch in front of his furnaces. Such gasworks were once a familiar sight in Scottish towns.

# D A L L A S
# D H U

People have made alchoholic drinks for thousands of years. Scotland's national drink is undoubtedly whisky, first recorded in literature in 1404. Most distilleries are found in the highlands and islands of Scotland. The best surviving historic malt distillery lies just south of Forres in Moray, Dallas Dhu. It was built in 1898/9 and continued distilling until 1983. The kiln (above) is recognisable from its distinctive shape.

# BROUGHTY
# CASTLE

The coasts of Scotland were repeatedly defended against invasion by England, France, The Netherlands, the United States of America, Russia and Germany. The eastern seaboard was particularly vulnerable and here most of the surviving defences are situated.

Broughty Castle at Dundee has seen much action in defence of Scotland since George Douglas, fourth Earl of Angus petitioned King James II in 1454 to erect a castle here. A naval war between Scotland and England about 1490 probably led to the re-building of the castle which was completed by 1496. In 1547 the English seized Broughty as part of their attempt to persuade Mary Queen of Scots to marry Edward Prince of Wales. After an occupation of two years it surrendered to joint Scots-French force and was thereafter garrisoned for a short time by the French.

By the late eighteenth century the castle was in ruins. It was another French threat which led to its renascence. The imperial ambitions of the Emperor Napoleon III were seen as dangerous for Britain. Broughty Castle had been purchased by the government in 1855 in order to build a fort to protect the Tay against Russian ships during the Crimean War. Now there was action and Robert Rowand (later Sir Rowand) Anderson restored the tower and built a coastal battery at its base in 1860–1. This fortification continued in use until World War II.

# INCHCOLM
# DEFENCES

The island of Inchcolm in the Firth of Forth boasts one of the best preserved medieval monasteries in Scotland. In both the World Wars the island was strongly defended to help protect the approaches to Edinburgh. Lookout posts and gun batteries of various dates dot the island.

Five hundred years earlier, Walter Bower, Abbot of Inchcolm, who died in 1449, wrote a history of Scotland entitled Scotichronicon. This is a major source of information for the early history of Scotland.

# DRYBURGH
# ABBEY

This simple stone at Dryburgh Abbey marks the grave of Earl Haig, commanding officer of the British army in France at the end of World War I and founder of the British Legion.

The people who erected the buildings described in this book are mostly unknown. However, at St Andrews the tombstone of a stonemason bears witness to the anonymous builders of Scotland's past.

# FURTHER READING

The Batsford/Historic Scotland series of books provide further information about many of the monuments and buildings featured in this book. They include:

Ian Armit, *Celtic Scotland*, 1997.

P J Ashmore, *Neolithic and Bronze Age Scotland*, 1996.

D J Breeze, *Roman Scotland, Frontier Country*, 1996.

R Fawcett, *Scottish Abbeys and Priories*, 1994.

R Fawcett, *Scottish Cathedrals*, 1997.

R Fawcett, *Stirling Castle*, 1996.

Sally Foster, *Picts, Gaels and Scots*, 1996.

Caroline Whickam-Jones, *Scotland's First Settlers*, 1994.

Iain MacIvor, *Edinburgh Castle*, 1993.

Anna Ritchie, *Viking Scotland*, 1993.

Anna Ritchie, *Prehistoric Orkney*, 1995.

C J Tabraham, *Scotland's Castles*, 1997.

C J Tabraham and Doreen Grove, *Fortress Scotland and the Jacobites*, 1995.

Val Turner, *Ancient Shetland*, 1998.

Peter Yeoman, *Medieval Scotland*, 1996.

From The Stationery Office :

Anna Ritchie ed., *Exploring Scotland's Heritage*, (series).

Anna Ritchie, *Scotland BC*, 1988.

Anna Ritchie and David J Breeze, *Invaders of Scotland*, 1991.

Anna Ritchie, *Picts*, 1989.

Christopher Tabraham, *Scottish Castles and Fortifications*, 1986.

Richard Fawcett, *Scottish Medieval Churches*, 1984.

David J Breeze, *A Queen's Progress*, 1987.

For a general history of Scotland, Michael Lynch's *Scotland, A New History* (Edinburgh 1995) can be recommended.

# ACKNOWLEDGEMENTS

I am grateful to colleagues for reading and commenting on this text: Dr Ian Armit, Mr Patrick Ashmore, Mr Gordon Barclay, Dr Richard Fawcett, Dr Noel Fojut, Mrs Marion Fry, Mrs Doreen Grove, Mrs Jackie Henrie, Dr Lesley Macinnes, Mr Graeme Munro, Ms Olly Owen and Mr Chris Tabraham. All the photographs are by Messrs Michael Brooks, David Henrie and Chris Hutcheson of the Historic Scotland Photographic Unit.

# FRIENDS OF HISTORIC SCOTLAND

Membership of the 'Friends' organisation gives free admission to over 300 Historic Scotland sites; half-price admission to English Heritage, Welsh Cadw and Manx National Heritage sites in the first year and free entry therafter; a free sites directory, full-colour quarterly magazine and other benefits; plus the satisfaction of contributing to the preservation of Scotland's built heritage for future generations. For further information write to Historic Scotland, Longmore House, Salisbury Place, Edinburgh EH9 1SH or telephone 0131 668 8600 (Main), 0131 668 8999 (Friends).

Details of all Historic Scotland properties can be found on the Website **www.historicscotland.gov.uk**

ORKNEY

Click Mill • • Gurness

Skara Brae •
Stenness • • Grain
Maes Howe

SHETLAND

• Mousa
Jarlshof

WESTERN
ISLES

• Black House, Arnol

• Calanais

Kinnaird Head

Duffus
Fort George • • Dallas Dhu • Duff House

INVERNESS

• Loanhead of Daviot

• Corgarff

ABERDEEN

Bridge of Oich

• Edzell

• Aberlemno

Eassie • Arbroath
Broughty • Ardestie

Dunstaffnage
Bonawe • • Kilchurn

Tullibardine • St Andrews

Eileach an Naiomh •

Kilmartin • Kinneil

Dunadd • Antonine
Achnabreck Wall Stirling • • Dunfermline
Inchcolm • Tantallon

Bearsden
Rothesay Dumbarton • Westquarter Prestonpans
Torphichen
EDINBURGH • Edin's Hall

Kildalton • Largs GLASGOW Cairnpapple
New Lanark Biggar Dryburgh • Smailholm
Douglas

Jedburgh

Crossraguel

Hermitage

Caerlaverock • Ruthwell
New Abbey

Threave

Whithorn

# PRACTICAL INFORMATION

Access to most of the 300 and more monuments in the care of Historic Scotland is free. At less than 70 there is an entry charge. From April to September, sites for which there is a charge are open Monday–Saturday 9.30–6.30pm, and Sunday 2.00pm–4.30pm. From October to March restricted openings apply and some properties close complete; opening hours normally are Monday–Saturday 9.30am–4.30pm. The last ticket is sold 30 minutes before closing.

Some monuments, in particular those on islands, can be difficult of access and visitors are recommended to consult the local tourist information office or the Historic Scotland guidebook.

The photographs in this book are available from Historic Scotland, Photographic Library, Longmore House, Salisbury Place, Edinburgh EH9 1SH or by telephone 0131 668 8647.

Guidebooks (and a catalogue) are also available to many of the monuments described in this book from Historic Scotland at the address above.

# HISTORIC SCOTLAND

**Arbroath Abbey**
Open all year

**Argyll's Lodging**
Open all year - see Stirling Castle for opening house and joint entry ticket details

**Black House, Arnol**
Closed every Sunday and all day Friday in winter.

**Bonawe Iron Furnace**
Open summer only.

**Bothwell Castle, Uddingston**
Closed Thursday pm and Friday in winter

**Caerlaverock Castle**
Open all year.

**Cairnpapple Hill**
Open summer only.

**Calanais Standing Stones & Visitor Centre**
Site open all year 7 days a week. Visitor Centre closed every Sunday. Summer from 10.00am to 7.00pm and winter 10.00am to 4.00pm

**Corgarff Castle**
Open summer and weekends in winter

**Crossraguel Abbey**
Open summer only.

**Dallas Dhu**
Closed Thursday pm and Friday in winter.

**Dryburgh Abbey**
Open all year

**Duff House**
Open all summer (except tuesday) from 10.00am to 5.00pm. Open Thursday to Sunday in winter 10.00am to 5.00pm.

**Dumbarton Castle**
Closed Thursday pm and Friday in winter.

**Dunfermline Abbey**
Closed Thursday pm and Friday in winter.

**Dunstaffnage Castle**
Open summer only.

**Edinburgh Castle**
Summer hours - All week 9.30am to 6.00pm. (last ticket sold 5.15pm) Winter hours - All week 9.30am to 5.00pm (last ticket sold 4.10pm)

**Edzell Castle**
Closed Thursday pm and Friday in winter.

**Fort George**
Open all year. Last ticket sold 45 minutes before closing.

**Gurness, Broch of**
Open summer only. Joint entry ticket for all Orkney monuments.

**Hermitage Castle**
Open summer only.

**Inchcolm Abbey**
Open summer only. Additional charge for ferry trip. Telephone 0131 331 4857 for details.

**Jarlshof**
Open summer only.

**Jedburgh Abbey**
Open all year.

**Kilchurn Castle**
Telephone 0131 668 8800

**Kinnaird Head Castle Lighthouse and Museum**
Open daily all year. Telephone 01346 511022 for further details.

**Maes Howe**
Open all year. Joint entry ticket for all Orkney monuments.

**New Abbey Corn Mill**
Closed Thursday pm and Friday in winter. Joint entry ticket with Sweetheart Abbey available.

**Rothesay Castle**
Closed Thursday pm and Friday in winter

**St Andrews Castle**
Open all year. Joint entry ticket with Cathedral available

**St Andrews Cathedral** (Museum and St Rule's Tower)
Open all year. Joint ticket available.

**Skara Brae**
Open all year. Joint entry ticket for all Orkney monuments.

**Smailholm Tower**
Open summer only.

**Stirling Castle**
Summer hours - all week 9.30am to 6.00pm (last ticket sold 5.15pm) Winter hours - all week 6.30am to 5.00pm (last ticket sold 4.15pm)

**Tantallon Castle**
Closed Thursday pm and Friday in winter.

**Threave Castle**
Open summer only. Charge includes ferry trip.

**Whithorn Priory**
Joint ticket by Whithorn Trust. Ticket gives entry to Priory, Priory Museum and archaeological dig.

# INDEX OF PLACES